The Complete Book About

Dodgeball

Including history, philosophy, strategies and games.

written and illustrated by
Andy Keyes

authorHOUSE™

1663 LIBERTY DRIVE, SUITE 200
BLOOMINGTON, INDIANA 47403
(800) 839-8640
WWW.AUTHORHOUSE.COM

First published by AuthorHouse 10/03/05

ISBN: 1-4208-7548-5 (sc)

Printed in the United States of America
Bloomington, Indiana

This book is printed on acid-free paper.

This book is dedicated to my
son and daughter.

I love you both.

Play is the work of children.
Don't ever grow up too much.

Special Thanks and Credit

This book could not be written without the help of many other important people. First and most important would be to thank my fellow teaching partners Rick Wickiser and Cris Cash for not only providing some of the games like *Gladiator* , *Cross Country Dodgeball* and *One Base Dodgeball*, but also for helping to refine and perfect all the games listed in this book. You are great teachers.

And the 5 young ladies who came up with *Fruit Salad* when they were in the 8th grade (you know who you are) have given us a game that will last for many years to come. Many classes of students have enjoyed playing the game you invented. Thanks!

I would also like to thank the World Dodgeball Association and the National Amateur Dodgeball Association for their cooperation and efforts to organize such a great game and for their support of this book.

Table of Contents

Diagrams

Forward

If you picked up this book then you are one of two types of people. You are either a fan of dodgeball and are curious to learn more or you hate dodgeball and can not believe that anyone would actually write a book about it. Which ever type you are you will find useful information in the rest of the book to support your position.

I am a Physical Education and Health teacher in Columbus, Ohio. I have been teaching for 14 years, and have taught all age groups from kindergarten to seniors. I received my Bachelor's Degree from Capital University and currently I am working on receiving a Master's Degree from Ashland University in Sport and Exercise Sciences. I have played dodgeball with all age groups and have had nothing but success. I am a firm believer that any game-properly structured-can be a positive experience for the students, parents and teacher. Bottom line on dodgeball is that kids will play the game with more enthusiasm than any other organized game. As a professional educator, I am will to do whatever it takes to get children moving for fun and fitness benefits. If dodgeball did not work I would not use it.

Andy Keyes

As you read this book you will find some history and theory related to dodgeball theory and a whole lot of different games. I will state up front that what is written in this book is nothing more than my opinion (shared by my fellow teaching partners) and should be viewed as such. I tried to set the book up so that it would an easy format to follow and humorous to read. I hope that you find the book enjoyable and useful in your pursuit to find games and activities that kids will actively participate in.

If you are an anti-dodgeball person you will still find plenty of good fuel for your fire within this book. Then again I might just make you a believer.

The Game of Dodgeball: The History

If you saw the movie <u>Dodgeball; A True Underdog Story</u> I hope that you do not think that the Chinese were the first to invent dodgeball by throwing human heads at one another. There is no basis in fact for that theory. Then again, if you did think that was real you probably missed the whole point of the movie anyway. I have done research into the true history of dodgeball and have come up with nothing. Seems no one has bothered to put down on paper when people first started throwing objects at one another for sport.

So if I have nothing in print to relate to then I will have to rely on what history tells us regarding humans and sport. Sport and competition have been around as long as the human race. The first sport for the earliest humans was merely to survive against the elements and nature. That would lead to battles over food, shelter, mates and territory. If one person or group had food then undoubtedly another would try to take it and a wrestling or boxing match would ensue. After a bit of time humans became more sophisticated in there approach to hunting by utilizing tools like spears, clubs, arrows and various methods of stone throwing. Today we still encourage these skills but only for sporting reasons-back then it was a matter of survival. But knowing human nature, it would not be surprising if perhaps a few hunters would get together and see who was a more accurate shot with a stone or arrow. Taking it a step further, it is no surprise that these same tools for providing food or leisure activities became tools for murder.

So how does dodgeball fit into this? Well suppose you had a group of hunters just sitting around one day with not much to do. Someone picks up a small stone, and out of boredom, throws it jokingly at his friend. His friend picks that same stone up and throws it back. Then another hunter throws one and another. Soon two teams form and they each find some shelter behind some trees or rocks and the first make shift dodgeball game is born. It was even better in the winter because the snow would not necessarily hurt as much as a stone would.

Why do children of today do the same thing? If you are a teacher then you will have seen this very scenario on a playground during recess. If you are a parent you will have seen it also, especially in the winter with snow. What child, at some point in their young lives, has not picked up snow, packed it into a ball shape and heaved it at someone or something. Older siblings will pick up toys and chuck them at younger brothers and sister for play and a means to say "back-off". Ironically, my daughter loves to throw her older brothers toys at him just to get him to chase her (one of her favorite games). Am I to assume that my daughter is doing this out of anger or spite, or rather a way to entice her brother into playing a game with her? I have to go with the game option here. I would have to say in most cases when dodgeball games organize on a playground or in a backyard they are for fun only with no intentions of hurting friends.

I am sure there is a psychologist somewhere who would argue against that point, but I have seldom met a psychologist who says one thing and another who will say the exact opposite to make a buck.

But let's go a step further and look at the history of sport in general. It can be argued that sport was develop as a way of fighting an enemy without necessarily using armies. The ancient Olympics were founded on this very principle. Ancient Greece was divided into several city-states that were always at war with each other. Every four years they would stop fighting and come together to compete in the Games. There was actually a law that forbid enemies from attacking one another while traveling to the games. (Punishment was severe if you were proven guilty of breaking this law.) The events of the original games were based upon war tactics and weapons. The chariot races, javelin throwing, boxing, wrestling and running events were all based upon necessary skills for fighting an enemy during times of war. So the Greeks took a violent exercise and turned it into acceptable sporting events for the masses to participate in or be a part of by watching them.

These same sports are practiced and cheered today even though they have barbaric roots.

Dodgeball is no more or less violent then any other sport. History tells us that humans participated in much more violent sport. Even our modern games of football, boxing, kickboxing, lacrosse, hockey and baseball have violent components to them.

They are acceptable, but dodgeball is not?!

In the next section I will compare dodgeball as a game to our more modern and civilized games.

Compared To Other Sports, Dodgeball Is......

One of the more common arguments is that Dodgeball is to violent and other sports can be used to teach the same skills-like throwing and catching. True, I do not disagree. Of course a goalie in any sport has to face the same situations as they would in a game of dodgeball. Football is not based on violence, but is a very violent sport by nature and it is taught in schools. Basketball has turned into more of a rough street game than the original game created by James Naysmith. Soccer has its own version of a "tackle" that will either take the ball away from an opponent or take an opponent out of the play. And what can be said about hockey-if you have ever watched a game I think you can agree that dodgeball is tame by comparison (at the professional level of course). Not that these are bad sports, I love to watch them, participate in them and teach them as well.

But with the increased TV coverage, what a student sees on TV is what they try to do on the field. I have seen and heard of students imitating "professional" wrestling as well. That has much greater potential for injury than dodgeball will ever. These same major sports are more rough today than 10 years ago and students are playing harder and more aggressive than 10 years ago.

Let's look at a few specific sports like football, soccer, lacrosse, water polo and volleyball. By comparing more traditional sports to dodgeball I will hopefully prove without a doubt that in no way is one any more violent than another. I will start with football.

Football is America's favorite sport. Surpassing even baseball as the greatest sport. I like to watch the NFL and college games on TV. I use to play endless hours of football after school and on weekends at my friend's house. We teach it at my school to sixth and seventh graders. There is no doubt that football is a staple in our society. But is it better to have an organized game of padded players whose job it is to tackle, with force, other players to keep a ball made of pigskin out of a certain area? Personally, I would rather get hit with a foam ball any day.

Football is a great sport, don't get me wrong. But if a school system is O.K. with allowing students to participate in such violence for months on end then why can't the rest of the student body participate in a more tame game? I say "tame" because compared to football, it is. Padded or not, there will always be more injuries on a football team then there will be in an entire student body participating in dodgeball. Why?

Because dodgeball does not have the contact element like football. When two body collide with enough force injury will be the result. Why is it that when running backs retire from the NFL they have mobility problems like bending and walking? Constant abuse of the joints and muscles will result in damage that can be permanent. In the 10+ years of teaching and playing dodgeball I know of 2 injuries and neither was life threatening or limiting in any way. Any football team should be so lucky to have the same statistic.

Soccer is another sport that is quite acceptable as a school sport but does have a violent and abusive component to it. As mentioned before there is the acceptable practice of "tackling"-sliding into an opposing player who has possession of the ball with the intent to get control of the ball. Key word here is "intent". I coached soccer for 5 years and watched as my players would sometimes get the ball and sometimes not, opting for the player instead. I never coached them to do that, but they learned it somewhere and brought it to the field.

And what of the goalie. If there is not a more paralleled position in soccer to dodgeball, I don't know what is. The goalies job in soccer, or any sport that has goalies for that matter, is to get behind the ball and stop it from going into the goal. The goalie may catch it, punch it, head it, kick it or use the any part of the body to stop the ball. It is not uncommon for the goalie to get bowled over in the process as well. The offensive player(s) comes rushing and wham-o, collision. Dodgeball has those same elements only without the collision part from opposing players. The ball is also much softer and less likely to leave bruises if hit by it.

In lacrosse it is legal to hit another player with your stick as long as it is above the waist and they have possession of the ball. In water polo it is not suppose to happen, but players will kick each other intentionally to gain better position in the pool. I am not sure but "dunking" another player is not suppose to happen either. And volleyball is the best because if you spike the ball hard enough the other team will not be able to return it. Of course it is even better when the ball is hit directly at an opposing player and bounces off with authority, maybe leaving a small tattoo resembling the ball manufacturer. All of the sports listed are school approved sports, all sports the school makes money off of and all sports that have greater risk of injury and are potentially more destructive than dodgeball.

Let's Play Dodgeball

I have ben teaching for 10+ years and have not found any game that students are more willing to participate in than dodgeball. They love it, they ask for it, they cheer when they learn we are going to play it and I do not have a lot of money invested in it either. The games are easy to set up and the rules are easy to follow. Even if a team loses they still have fun playing. My students who will generally do nothing in any other unit will get involved with dodgeball.

I once asked a group of students who were more into "alternative sports" (skateboarding, inline skating, etc.) why they loved dodgeball but never really seemed to get involved in soccer or softball units. The response was because it is a game that adults have not overtaken and made to structured, thus taking away the "fun" of just playing. (I paraphrased for the sake of keeping the language understandable.) This makes sense to me because the level of participation in nontraditional sports is on the rise in America as our youth try find activities that anyone can do for fun without a lot of rules and adult supervision and that let them express themselves as they see fit. Face the fact-Dodgeball is for the masses because it is fun and anyone can participate whether they are athletically gifted or not.

I am not saying that dodgeball will work as a motivation tool for all students. I too have students who will not put any effort into class regardless of what we are playing. And it does not come from a lack of trying either. I have set up units where the students choose from a long list of options and they still do not put in any effort. But as a game compared to all others-I will have a higher percentage of participation across the board with any of the dodgeball games versus any other game. I have seen it time and time again in all possible settings.

Getting back to my point, students love to play dodgeball. And with the huge rise in childhood obesity and Type II Juvenile Diabetes in this country we had better be finding something for our youth to get involved in or we face a future with a lot adults dying of heart attacks. If you can get the students interested in playing any game, they are going to be more willing to try other sporting activities that will foster a life long habit of exercising. That is my goal and it should be the goal of any physical educator.

So how should a teacher go about accomplishing this in a school? The first place to start is with the ball.

The Ball:

I am not a supporter of using the old playground style rubber balls. I grew up using these types of balls and can remember many times leaving class with red marks. I did not mind it personally but can understand why someone would not want to play with that type of ball. Funny thing is when I see news stories on 60 Minutes or HBO about dodgeball the teacher is still using this type of ball. No wonder there is still a bad rap about dodgeball.

In any physical education equipment catalog you will find a section devoted to dodgeballs. They come in many sizes and a whole rainbow of color options. I myself (as well as my fellow teachers) are partial to the neon green and orange ones. These balls are made of a low density foam and coated with a thin rubber to prevent tearing. Using these balls reduces any risk of being hurt when a student gets hit. Even balls that hit the face will do no more damage than make the eye water. The newer balls are not heavy enough and are to soft to cause any bruising. I am not a doctor-but I have never had a serious injury in my gym while playing dodgeball with any student. The worst injury I have had to date is when a student bend down to pick up a ball and hit his nose on his knee and it bled. (Can any football team make the same claim?)

The equipment a teacher chooses to use in any unit should be the safest possible and of the highest quality. These balls are marketed specifically for dodgeball for a reason-they are safe! Or maybe I am wrong and the supply companies are wrong and don't realize that they are selling products with huge injury potential. Of course these same companies sell archery equipment as well. (Didn't we use archery at one time as a weapon and for hunting defenseless animals and keeping the enemy away?)

Let me make this point perfectly clear-**NO ONE SHOULD EVER USE THE RUBBER PLAYGROUND BALLS FROM THE 70's AND 80's.** Any ball used for dodgeball should be made of a low density foam with a thin rubber coating. These balls come in a large range of sizes. Typical size is an 8 1/2 inch diameter ball. 81/2" is a perfect size for high school or adults to use. I use a 7 inch ball for my middle school students and found that is works much better. The 7" ball is easier for small hands to grip, it is easier to throw and it also holds up better throughout an entire school year. I would typically buy a dozen new 8 1/2" dodgeballs every year. With the 7" I only have to purchase 4-6. I believe it is because the kids do not try to hold the ball with fingernails-it is small enough for hands. I will say it is a bit harder to catch a smaller ball, but it does re-enforce proper catching techniques. I see huge improvements in catching ability in other games like kickball and flag football because of dodgeball.

I would not go any smaller than a 7" ball though. You can purchase smaller ones, all the way down to baseball size. But the problem becomes one of how hard a student can throw it. The smaller the ball the faster it goes. The 7" is the smallest diameter size I believe anyone should use for safety sake.

Standard Rules For Any Game:

Each game listed in this book will have different rules. You may not be allowed to catch a ball (Gladiator) or cross a line (Tournament Dodgeball) or even get back in a game unless a team mate hits an object (Net dodgeball and Pin Dodgeball). But all the games listed in this book do have some rules that are standard. I call them "normal dodgeball rules" when introducing a new game to students or telling them what game they are playing that day. My fellow teachers and I have established these rules to prevent injury and unnecessary rough play. They are as follows:

1. You can only get another player out by hitting them shoulders to feet. Loose shirts and shorts do count as part of the body.

2. Hitting another player in the head never counts as an out.

3. If a player from the opposing team catches a thrown ball in the air, the player who threw the ball is out.

4. Players are not allowed to cross boundary lines.

5. A ball is considered free (safe to pick up) once it hits any other object like the floor, a wall, a backboard or another player.

6. If a ball hits a player and another player from the same team catches the ball, the player hit is out. If the player hit catches a ball that bounce up off of them then the thrower is out. (This rule can vary from teacher to teacher, but I use it so students learn to track the ball and try to make a play.)

7. Students are not allowed to hold on to a ball for more than 5 seconds.

The games listed in this book are taken from years of playing and teaching. Some you may be familiar with and others may seem completely unreal. I have adapted old games and given new rules to them. I have taken completely different games from movies and turned them into a game and there is even a game that our own students made up themselves as part of a project. Feel free to adapt any game to your specific needs. The important thing is to make sure all involved are having fun-and that is the easy part.

How To Start A Game:

To start a game I have tried lots of different formats. The one I use the most for safety sake is to have players against a wall and pick 1 person from each team to be a "paddler". All the balls are in the middle of the gym and on the signal the paddlers run to the middle and try to paddle as many balls as possible to their side of the gym. When all balls are on a side then play may begin on the second signal. Be aware to warn students to not slide or dive into the balls. The potential for a collision exists with the excitement of starting this way.

The other start I use is to place an equal number of balls a few feet in front of each team. On a signal the game starts and the students can pick up a ball and start throwing. This works well because those who would rather catch balls don't have to worry about moving up front right away. This type of start is good when students are restricted to one half of a gym or playing area. *(See Diagram 1 and 2,)*

A simple easy start to use is to simply throw out an equal number of balls to each

team before starting. It is not glamorous, but it does work. When I use this start I will give the loosing team all the balls before starting the next game.

The other exceptions to these starting formats are listed in the following games: Gladiator, Elimination, Team Elimination,

Final Four Elimination, Scatter Dodge Ball, Quidditch, Medic/ Doctor Dodge Ball and Fruit Salad. The starts for these games are included in the description of each game.

Of course, use whatever works best for you and your students. There are no limits to how any game can begin. Experiment and see what happens. Just keep safety in the front of your mind and you may discover something better than what I currently use.

Play Time:

This is the easy part of setting up any game(s). No matter what game you set up you will not have a hard time keeping the students motivated. The best thing dodgeball has going for itself is the fact that it is flat out fun. My students love to play no matter how I set up the game. I can change the rules up in the middle of a game, restrict playing space, take away balls or whatever and the students still have a fun time playing. The only negative thing I can say about dodgeball is that there are times when I have to disappoint students by not playing it. Math and science should be so lucky.

In the games that follow I have described how I have set up the games and what I have found works best for me. When you do decide to play any game be sure to account for the amount of equipment you have available, the space you have to play in and the number of students in your class. Some games require a substantial amount of equipment (Gladiator and Quidditch for instance) and if you do not have what I suggest to use you may have to come up with safe alternatives. Class size and available playing space are also going to dictate what you can and can not do.

I can not stress enough though how important it will be for you to consider safety. Change any game to fit your needs, but think through as many injury possibilities that you can and account for them. If you have portable volleyball poles in the corner of your gym, make that a "no play zone". If you have bleachers that are out or partially out, restrict the playing area to avoid those areas. If you are outside, be a cautious of fences, trees, bushes, parking lots, etc. that may interfere with your game and student safety.

But no matter how you set up a game your students will have a great time playing-I guarantee it!

The Games

What follows are the games that I have my students play. Each game listed includes the equipment needed, set up and rules for play. Some of the games also have variations listed at the end. They are in no specific order. Please feel free to change any game to meet your needs and expectations. Have fun and be safe!

Note that most of the games require a place for "out" players to go. My gym has bleachers along one wall which work great for me. I just pull out the first row for the students to sit on. If you do not have bleachers you can always use cones to mark off an area or even designate one wall as a place to go. Keep in mind that whatever method you choose to make sure the students are always in you line of sight. This is important in games like *Net Dodgeball* where team members get back in a game once a net is hit-you can let them know when they are free to reenter the game.

The Start:

I have included two diagrams for starting the games. They are only options, but you may want to try them first and then develop your own ideas. I like them because they are simple and once the students get to know them it is easier to get games started because all you have to do tell them to get to a wall and your ready to go. Please see Diagrams #1 and #2 for complete set up.

Diagram #1

Starting a game using a **paddler** from each team.

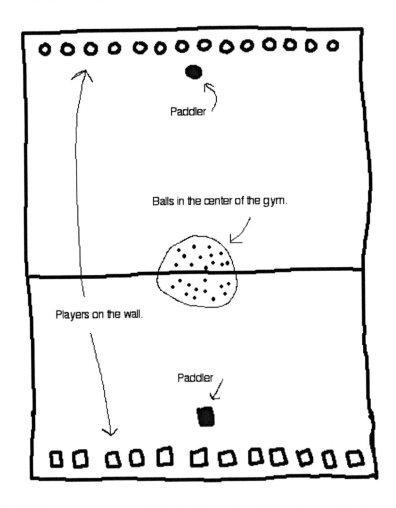

Paddler

Balls in the center of the gym.

Players on the wall.

Paddler

Diagram #2

Starting a game with the balls divided between both teams.

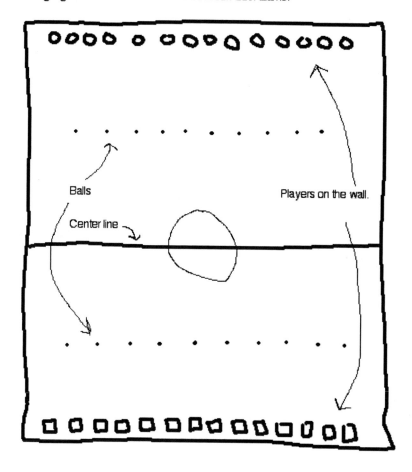

Balls

Players on the wall.

Center line

Original Dodgeball

Equipment:

12 - 16 dodge balls, gym or any open space (preferably with walls)

Set Up:

Divide class into 2 groups on each side of gym. *(See Diagram 3)*

Play:

This is a very simple game to play. Players must stay on their side of the gym. They may throw a ball from anywhere on their half of the gym to get opposing players out. The player's objective is to knock out every member of the other team. A player is out only if he/she gets hit with a ball between the shoulders and feet or if an opposing player catches a ball in the air that was thrown at them then the thrower is out. Players may use a ball to block a ball that is thrown at them. Out players sit on the side of the gym or in a designated area until a new game starts. Any ball that hits another object (the floor, walls, ceiling, backboard or another player) is considered a free ball. Play continues until only one team is left.

Variations:

After a designated signal, players may run anywhere in the gym and chase opposing players to get them out. This works well when there are only 2 or 3 players left on each team and no one wants to take a chance on throwing a ball. This also works well when all the balls end up on one side of the gym and that team is not throwing anything back.

Making the play area bigger by having a "neutral zone", where either team may play from, is fun also. I also put in the "blocking" rule. A player may block a ball while holding a ball but if that ball gets knocked out of his/her hands then they are out (they must maintain control of the ball).

Diagram #3

Original Dodgeball

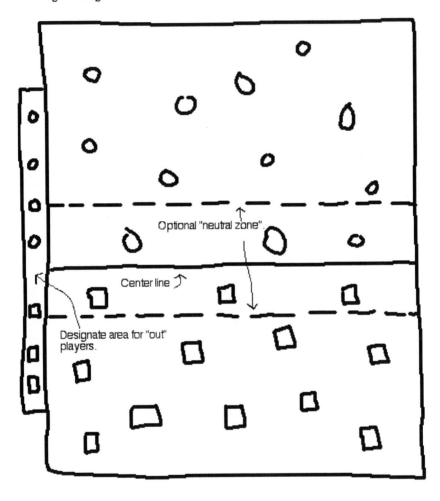

Net Dodgeball

12-16 dodge balls, gymnasium with basketball hoops and nets

Set Up:

Divide class into 2 equal teams. Each team is assigned to one half of the gym. *(See Diagram 4)*

Play:

The basic dodge ball rules apply. If a player is hit from shoulders to feet they are out, a ball caught in the air results in the thrower being out and any ball that hits another object is a free ball. Out players must sit in a designated area. Play continues until only one team is left. (See Original Dodgeball)

The twist in this game is that "out" players may get back in if one of their team mates hits a net on the opposing teams side of the gym. When a net is hit then all players for that team are allowed to get back in the game. Only the net counts-rims and backboards are no good.

This game may last for quite a while and you may never get one team to actually win. If one team does win then a whole new game starts with everyone back in. Keeping track of how many games each team wins makes it interesting for players.

Variation:

You can declare a team a winner if they get a ball through a basket. The gym I use has three baskets per side so I use the center basket since it is the farthest away.

Another fun variation is to have a "neutral zone" that any player can enter. This is a good way to get opposing players out by simply tagging them with a ball instead of throwing it at them. I also use the center basket only since the playing area is larger.

Diagram #4

Net Dodgeball

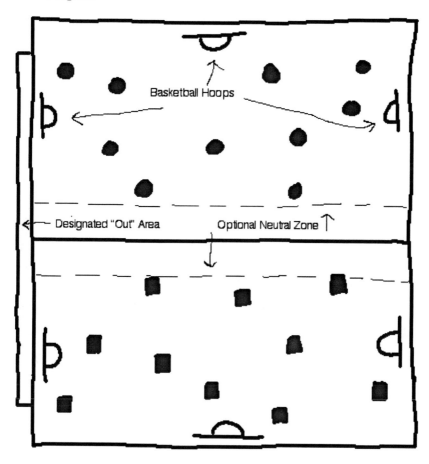

Bombardment

12 - 16 dodgeballs, gymnasium

Set Up:

Divide group into two equal teams. Each team is assigned to one half of the gym. *(See Diagram 5)* I recommend using the "Paddler Start" for this game.

Play:

Basic dodgeball rules apply. If a player is hit shoulders to feet with a ball they are out. If a ball is caught in the air the thrower is out. A ball that hits any other object is a free ball. (See Original Dodgeball.)

This game requires constant awareness of what is going on around the gym. Players must watch for balls from the opponents side and from behind them as well. The objective is to get all players out on the opposing team. The fun in this game is that even when a player is "out", they are not. Any player who is "out" must go to the other side of the gym (opponent's side) and stand against the wall behind a predetermined line. "Out" players may get back to their side of the gym by hitting an opposing player with ball. "Out" players may pick up any ball that comes in the Out Zone (they may not come onto the floor to get one) or a team mate may try to throw a ball to them.

This is a game that can last for a long time, so no team may win for quite awhile.

Andy Keyes

Diagram #5

Bombardment

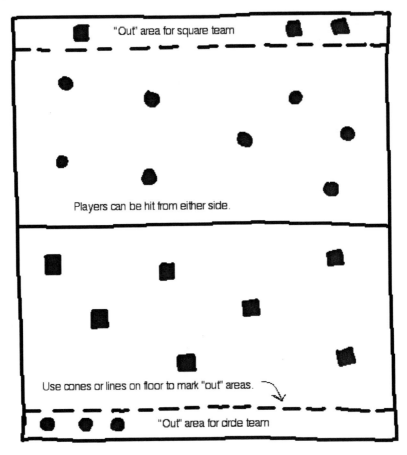

30

Elimination

6-8 dodgeballs, gymnasium

Set Up:

In this game there are no teams, it is everyone for himself or herself. There needs to be a designated "out" area. *(See Diagram 6)*

Play:

Everyone spreads out in the gym. Play starts when the teacher throws out the balls. (It would be a good idea to throw out the balls and if a player catches one they must hold it until a signal is given to start play. That way players without a ball have time to move away from the ball.) Regular rules apply. If you are hit shoulders to feet you are out, if a player catches a ball the thrower is out and head shots never count. Players without a ball may move anywhere in gym. If someone has a ball they can not move with it. They can throw it and try to get someone out or drop it and move on. Anyone can pick up any loose ball and try to get someone out. If a player (player 1) gets out they go to the designated "out" area. When player 2 (the one who got player 1 out) gets out then player 2 sits out and player 1 gets back in the game. (Players may not always know who got them out so the teacher may have to pick someone for that player to watch to get out so they get back in the game.) Play continues until only one player remains. Any 2 or more players caught teaming up automatically have to sit out until a player, picked by the teacher, gets out.

Variations:

Players may change position in gym while holding a ball only if they roll it on the ground and pick it back up in a new location. Any ball on the floor is a free ball though.

This is a game that has no ending. In the 10+ years of playing it I have never had anyone win. Kids love trying though and it gets very competitive.

Diagram #6

Elimination Dodgeball

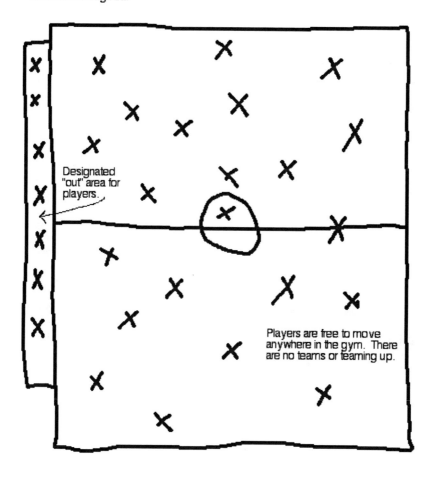

Designated "out" area for players.

Players are free to move anywhere in the gym. There are no teams or teaming up.

Team Elimination

Same set up as Elimination (see Diagram #6) except each player will have a partner to work with. Players may pass ball to each other and try to get into positions to get other players out. Same rules apply as all other games. If one player from a team gets out the other player of that same team is still in the game.

This is a good version to teach cooperation and team work. You will also find that the game moves a bit faster and there will most likely be a winning team, unlike Elimination. Students seem to like this version because it gives them the opportunity to work with another player as opposed to being against all other players.

You can always try teams of three or four if you have larger classes. The difference will be the strategy used by the players. I have found that with more than 2 players partnered up, 1 player will rely on the others to do all the work. It is still a fun way to play Elimination, just different.

Final Four Elimination

Equipment:

4 dodgeballs, gymnasium

Set Up:

This is like Elimination. It is everyone against everyone. There are no teams or teaming up. *(See Diagram 6)*

Play:

Play starts when the teacher throws out the four balls. Players must hold ball until teacher gives signal to start, that allows for the other players to move away from the balls. Regular rules apply, if a player is hit between the shoulders and feet they are out, a ball caught in the air results in the thrower getting out and head shots never count. Players may relocate in the gym by rolling ball on ground and picking it back up. Once a player is out they sit in designated "out" area until new game starts. When only 4 players are left the game stops briefly so that each player can get a ball. When play resumes players may run with ball in hand until only 1 player is left. Games last around 3-5 minutes so no one will sit out for very long.

This is a great game for players of various athletic ability. A player may elect to not pick up a ball until they are 1 of the final 4. The "non-athletic" players will like it because it gives them a chance to sneak up on anyone and get them out (which is a rather common thing in this game). I have more "non athletes" winning this game than the "athletes" most of the time because they do such a good job of avoiding getting hit. Strategy is key in this game.

If you are working with large classes you can always add a 5th ball to speed things up. Just make sure there is adequate space to play.

Pin Dodgeball

Equipment:

12-16 dodgeballs, 6 bowling pins or Indian clubs or something that can be set up and knocked over by a ball

Set Up:

Divide into 2 equal teams, each on 1 half of the gym. Each team will have 3 pins on their half of the gym about 10 feet or so from the wall (spread them a part to make it more difficult for the opposition). *(See Diagram 7)*

Play:

Normal dodgeball rules apply. A hit between shoulders and feet, player is out, catch a ball in the air and the thrower is out, head shots never count, "out" players sit in designated area. The objective in this game is to knock over the center pin to win. If a pin on the outside is knocked over then all players from the team that knocked it over get back in the game. Outside pins may be set back up after being knocked over. Players may protect their pins, but only 1 player may protect a pin at any time. Protectors of pins may not hold a ball and if they accidentally knock a pin over it counts the same as if the other team knocked it over. Protectors may catch balls but have to get rid of them right away.

This is a good game to re-enforce bowling skills and accurate throwing.

Variation:

The first team to knock over all pins wins.

Diagram #7

Pin Dodgeball

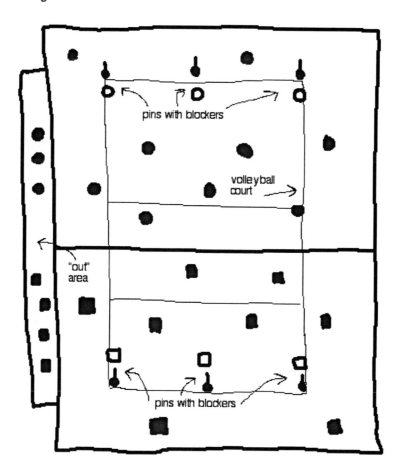

pins with blockers

volleyball court

"out" area

pins with blockers

Kamikaze Dodgeball

12 - 16 dodgeballs, basketball court, 2 suspended hula hoops.

Set Up:

Divide the players into 2 equal teams each on one half of the court. The suspended hoops can be hung up anywhere at one end of the gym in line with the basketball hoops. You can hang them vertically or I prefer horizontally about 4 to 5 feet higher then the basketball hoop.

(Suspended Hoop Idea: I attached a basketball net to a hula-hoop with some zip-ties and then used some string to hang it from the rafters in the gym. To get it up there I tied one end of the string to a tennis ball and tossed the ball up in the rafters where I wanted to hang the hoop from then just hauled it up to the desired height. The hoop also comes in handy when teaching basketball to younger students because you can make the hoop as high as you like.) *(See Diagram 8)*

Play:

Normal dodgeball rules apply.   Any player hit below shoulders is out. A thrown ball that is caught gets the thrower out. Head shots never count. Out players sit in designated area.

The objective in this game is for a player from one side to cross over to opponent's side of the court to get a ball thru the suspended hoop. The first team to do this wins. (This is the Kamikaze part because it usually means sacrificing for your team.) If a player wants to he/she can shoot a ball thru the basketball hoop to get their team mates back in the game.

Any player on the other side of the court can not get an opponent out. They can catch a ball to stay alive, but that is all other than shooting at a hoop. If they get hit trying to shoot then they are out. If the ball is released before the player gets hit then the shot is good if it makes it thru any hoop.

Players may protect their hoop either with a ball or by blocking someone from getting close to a hoop. Players may also try a long shot from their side of the gym to win or get players back in the game.

This is a very strategic game. Players have to take on specific roles to either play offense or defense. Play is usually slow the first few games but picks up after they learn how to play. Kids love this game especially when it get down to only a few players and they scramble to get a ball thru the hoop to win.

Variation:

If you do not want to mess with the suspended hoops you can always use basketball hoops. In my gym I will use the side hoops to get players back in and the center to win a game.

If your gym only has one court you can use different colored balls for different bonuses. Example: red balls in a hoop get players back in and a yellow ball in a hoop will win a game. Any color will work and you can limit how many balls will get players in or win a game. Give each team one red and yellow ball and the rest can be another color used to get individual players out.

Diagram #8

Kamikazee Dodgeball

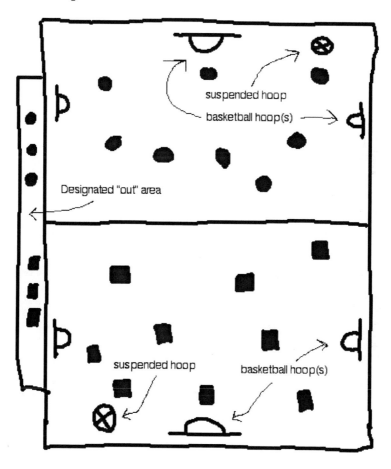

Gladiator Dodgeball

Equipment:

12 -16 dodgeballs, gymnasium, 4 - 6 folding mats, 4 pineys/ jerseys, 8 or more cones

Set Up:

Set the cones up in the center of the gym. Place mats on edge around the outer part of the gym but away from the walls. Use 2 on the sides and 1 at each end. Divide players into 2 equal teams. 1 team will be on the outside and the other will be inside the cones. The inside team will need 4 people to wear pineys. *(See Diagram 9)*

Play:

The objective of this game is to score as many runs as possible for as long as possible. The outside team (A) runs around the perimeter of the gym as many times as possible without getting hit by a ball. The inside team (B) tries to get outside players out by hitting them below the shoulders. If an "A" player catches a ball he/she is out. "Out" players sit a designated area until time expires. "B" players may not leave the center of the gym. Retrievers (those wearing the pineys) are to move around gym and throw balls back into the center so "B" players can throw the balls again. Members of the "A" team can hide behind a mat but only for 5 seconds, then they must move on. Play should last for 3-5 minutes. Count the number of outside players left, that is their score. The other option is to count each time players cross a "score line" and add up the number of points after time expires. Switch teams, pick new retrievers and start again. Repeat as often as possible.

This is a great cardiovascular workout for everyone. Players will sweat a lot.

This is also a great opportunity to talk about the history of the Roman Empire, gladiators and the Colosseum.

Andy Keyes

Diagram #9

Gladiator Dodgeball

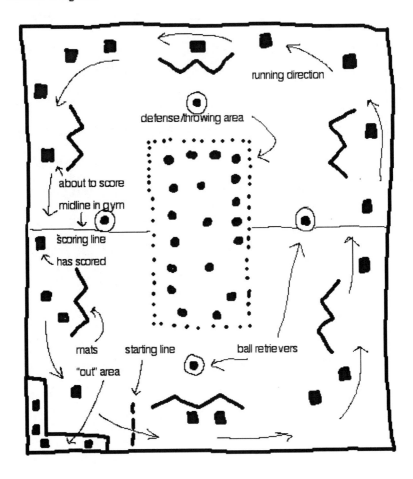

46

Scatter Dodgeball

Equipment:

4 - 6 dodgeballs, gymnasium

Set Up:

Players spread themselves out in the gym. There are no teams. *(See Diagram 6)*

Play:

The teacher throws out the balls. If a player gets one they must hold on to it until the signal is given to start play. Other players may scatter away from the balls before play starts. Once play begins players try to get others out by hitting them with a ball below the shoulders or catching a thrown ball. Players with a ball may not move with it, but they can relocate their position in the gym by rolling the ball or tossing it against a wall and catching it again. Any loose ball can be picked up by any other player. If a player gets out they sit in a designated area until a new game starts. Play does not stop until only one player is left.

This is a fast paced game. The nice thing about this is everyone is equal-anyone can get out at any time. The more athletic players typically will be the first to go because they are too aggressive.

Medic Dodgeball (Doctor Dodgeball)

Equipment:

12 - 16 dodgeballs, 6 folding mats, 2 pineys

Set Up:

Divide players into 2 equal teams. Each team gets half of the gym. Each team may set up 3 folding mats anywhere on their side for protection (encourage them to set them up on end so they have more to hide behind). Each team needs to pick one person to wear the piney-they will be the medic. Each team starts with an equal number of balls. *(See Diagram 10)*

Play:

The objective of this game is to hit the medic with a ball to win the game. Normal dodgeball rules apply in this game. If a player gets "out" then they must sit down right where the "out" occurred. To get back in the medic has to tag or touch them.

Once tagged a player is allowed to resume playing. The medic can move freely around their half of the gym. Anyone can hide behind the mats for protection. The medic may have 1 body guard-but if the body guard gets out then they have to sit down like everyone else. A body guard is not allowed use a ball to block thrown balls.

When a medic gets hit then play stops and each team picks new medics to start a new game. It is a good idea to rotate medics by having a boy pick a new girl medic then the girl picks a new boy medic.

Variations:

You can put the medic on scooters and have a body guard push them around the gym to get players back in the game. Kids love this, but warn them about rolling over fingers!

Diagram #10

Medic/ Doctor Dodgeball

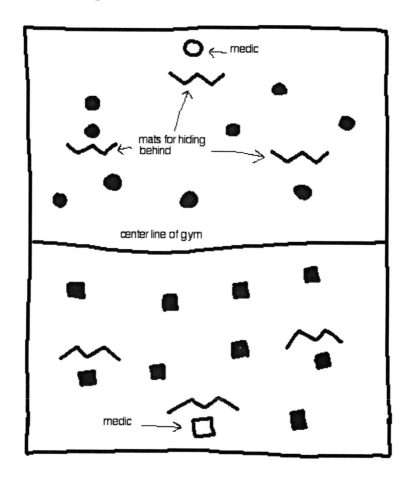

center line of gym

Fruit Salad

Equipment:

4 sets of different colored pineys, 10 dodgeballs - 5 sets of the same color (example: 2 red, 2 blue, 2 orange, 2 yellow and 2 green)

Set Up:

Divide players into 4 equal teams and assign each team to a corner of the gym and assign them a colored piney to wear to match their ball color. Place 2 balls (same color) in back of each team different than the team color. *(See Diagram 11)*

Play:

The objective of this game is to be the last team standing. Normal dodgeball rules apply. Each team starts in a corner of the gym. On the signal players may run out and try to pick up their colored balls only. Players may only use the balls that match their piney to get other players out. If a player catches another teams ball then the thrower is out and the catcher must drop the ball immediately. Players may move freely throughout the gym. When a player is out they sit in a designated area until a new game starts. Any player may use the "bonus" balls to get other players out. (Throw them out whenever you like. Make sure the "bonus" balls do not match any other teams balls.) Players may not run with a ball. To change locations they must pass ball to another player. When only one player is left on a team that player may roll ball on ground to change locations.

Kids love this game. All abilities can play and the athletes do not always win. There is a lot of cooperation and strategy involved so players have to learn how to work together to succeed. This is a game designed by 8th grade students. They came up with it so they could play a game that they would have "fun" playing so you can't go wrong with it.

Variations:

If you want to divide teams up to make them smaller then just make sure there are enough different colored piney and balls. We have played with five teams before-we have one team without piney and it worked real well. The fifth team just starts against a wall and we move the balls past the center of the gym so it is a fair start. *(see Diagram 11)*

Diagram #11

Fruit Salad

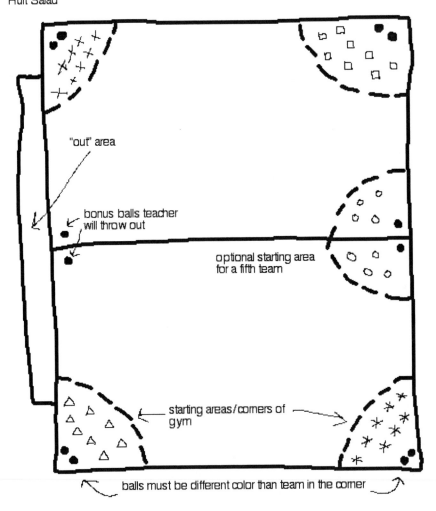

"out" area

bonus balls teacher will throw out

optional starting area for a fifth team

starting areas / corners of gym

balls must be different color than team in the corner

One Base Dodgeball

Equipment:

2 dodgeballs, 3 cones, 1 base, 6 piney any color

Set Up:

Divide group into 2 teams. One team will line up at one end of the gym (offense) and the other will spread out randomly in the gym (defense). The base should be placed near the offensive team and the cone at the other end of the gym. Place the other 2 cones at a corner of the gym where the runners will start. The first 6 runners will wear the piney. _(See Diagram 12)_

Play:

Two or 3 offensive players will line up between starting cones. The teacher will throw out the 2 dodgeballs. The runners must run around the cone at the other end of the gym and then touch the base before getting hit with the ball. Runners may go anywhere in the gym necessary to avoid getting hit while trying to score. Once they get out or score a run then the next runner starts. There should always be 2 or 3 people trying to score-continuous play is a must for this game. (Teachers will want to keep an eye on the runners to make sure there are always 2 running at the same time.) The defensive players want to keep people from scoring by getting them out. If any offensive player is hit shoulders to feet with a ball then they are out. Defensive players may not run with a ball. They must pass the ball in order to get a better position to make an out.

Once the entire offensive line has had a chance to run and score then teams switch sides.

Variations/Suggestions:

It is a good idea to designate an area around the base that defensive players can not come in to get a runner out. They may come in to get a ball but it must be passed back out in order to get someone out. We use the 3 point arch on the gym floor. It is also a good idea to have the offensive people who are running wear piney so that they are easier to find on the floor. Once they get out or score they give their piney to the next runner in line.

To get the ladies more involved you can always make the rule that ladies can get anyone out-guys can only get guys. Or you can make it guys get the guys out and girls get girls out.

If you have large groups of people and want smaller teams then make 3 or 4 teams but only 1 is trying to score at a time, the other 3 work together to keep the scores low. This is a good way to teach cooperation.

This is a great game that moves real fast and gets everyone involved. Students will be sweating after this one.

This game also works very well outside on a soccer field or football field. The cones can be spread farther apart and the extra space makes for a more challenging game. The students will get a very good cardiovascular workout!

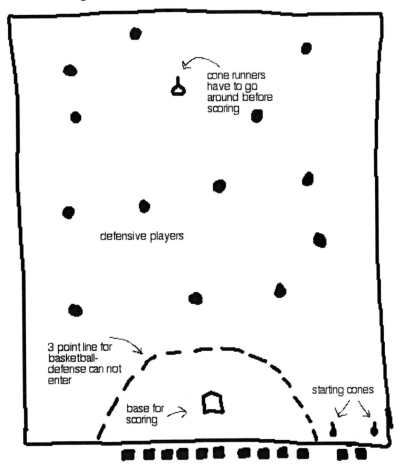

Diagram #12

One-Base Dodgeball

cone runners
have to go
around before
scoring

defensive players

3 point line for
basketball-
defense can not
enter

starting cones

base for
scoring

offense/runners on the wall

Soccer Dodgeball

Equipment:

6 - 8 dodgeballs, piney (if needed)

Set Up:

You can set this up a couple of different ways. Split the group into 2 separate teams, separate into 4 smaller teams or no teams, everyone plays for themselves. *(See Diagram 13)*

Play:

Depending on how you wish to set this up some creativity may be in order. But the basic rules would remain the same. If you have a ball your objective is to kick the ball soccer style (inside or outside of foot) at another player to get them out. Any player hit below the knees or the feet is out, body and head shots do not count. (This ensures that the ball stays low to the ground.) Out players would go sit in a designated area until a new game starts. If you do not have a ball you are free to move anywhere in the playing area to avoid getting hit.If using a team format, players on the same team may pass the ball between them to try to get someone out. Players can not move the ball by dribbling it though, this cuts down on more advanced players getting off really hard shots. *(See Diagram 3)*

If you have a 2 or 4 team formation, the last team standing wins. If it is everyone against everyone, when only 1 person is left that person wins. *(Similar set up as "Fruit Salad". See Diagram 11)*

If you prefer small groups of players, say 6-8 players, it is fun to have them circle up and one player is in the middle. The players on the outside pass the ball around and then try to hit the center player below the knees. The center player may run around the inside to get away from the ball. Whoever hits the middle player switches places and they become the center player. The player who avoids getting hit the longest wins. *(See Diagram 13)*

This is a great way to stress the importance of making good passes and trapping.

When players are in the middle they are getting plenty of exercise while trying not to get hit.

Variations:

Trapping can be like catching a ball in a regular game. Any ball that is successfully trapped with the foot or knee results in the player who kicked it being out. Be prepared to make a lot of judgment calls with this though.

You could play this like Doctor Dodgeball and designate 1 person from each team as a "Goalie". If the opposing team hits the other team's goalie then all out players for that team get back in. This is only good for 1 time per game because the goalie can not get back in once out. This works well for a 2 team set up.

When playing the everyone for themselves version it is fun to have players get back in when the person that got them out gets out. This becomes a never ending game that no one can win unless one person can get all other players out. (See Elimination Dodgeball)

This is a great soccer lead up activity or concluding activity to a soccer unit. Students love playing it and as long as soccer balls are not used so the risk of injury is low.

Diagram #13

Soccer Dodgeball

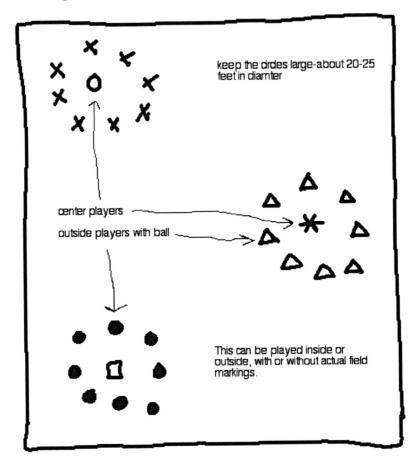

keep the circles large-about 20-25 feet in diamter

center players

outside players with ball

This can be played inside or outside, with or without actual field markings.

Quidditch

Equipment:

6 dodgeballs (2 sets of the same color), 1 small ball (a mini soccer ball or playground ball would do), piney, 6 hoop goals, 4 cones, and 1 really small ball (a ping-pong ball would work)

Set Up:

See diagram for court set up. Our hoop goals are made from PVC pipe purchased at a hardware store-a very cheap way to make goals. Divide group into 2 different teams. 1 team will wear piney. 1 player from each team will wear a different color piney from the rest of the players (chasers). Each team will have players on the court and some on the sides so each team will have to be divided again. Each sub-team will play both on and off the court though. *(See Diagram 14)*

Play:

Credit must be given to the *Harry Potter* novels and movies for this game. It is to bad we can't all be on flying brooms or this would be a much more interesting game to play.

Half of each team will start on the court on their side of the field. The other half of each team will be spread out on their side line with the dodgeballs. 1 player on each sidelines will be designated retriever for their team. Each team may designate 1 player on the court as a goalie.

To start play the teacher/referee will toss the small ball (quaffle) into the air, like a jump ball. Players on the court then try to gain possession of the ball and pass to their team mates and score. Players may not run with the ball. They may have a step to pass or shoot the ball. A goal is scored when the ball passes through any hoop. Goals are worth 1 point each. After a goal is scored the goalie throws the quaffle to a team mate to continue play. The defensive team may try to intercept any ball or block a pass or shot. Any ball on the ground can be picked up by anyone on the court.

The players on the sideline use the dodgeballs (bludgers) to get players from the other team out on the court. Any player that is hit shoulders to feet must join the sideline team for that rotation. Players on the sidelines may only use the color ball assigned to them. One player from each team on the side will need to be a "retriever" so that they can pass "bludgers" back to their sideline.

When ever the teacher/referee is ready they can toss the really small ball (golden snitch) onto the court. Once the snitch is released the designated chaser from each team tries to get control of the snitch and score a goal. No one but chasers may touch the snitch-but others on the court may kick it to their chaser or away from an opposing chaser. A goal scored with the snitch is worth 10 points. I use an Odd Bounce ball as our snitch. It is nice because is does not react the same as a round ball. Odd Bounce balls can be purchased from any Phys. Ed. supply company.

Players have 4 - 6 minutes to play then rotate with team on sidelines. Different chasers and goalies may be assigned each rotation as well.

Andy Keyes

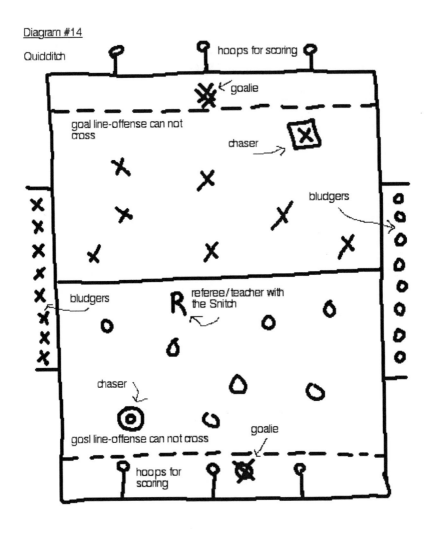

Diagram #14

Quidditch

hoops for scoring

goalie

goal line-offense can not cross

chaser

bludgers

bludgers

referee/teacher with the Snitch

chaser

gosl line-offense can not cross

goalie

hoops for scoring

Cross Country Dodgeball

Equipment:

6-10 dodgeballs (old ones would work best due to track surface), track

Set Up:

Pick 6-10 people to start with a ball (depending on how many balls you are using).

The rest of the class is about 10-15 yards ahead of them on the track. *(See Diagram 15)*

Play:

On the signal from the teacher the ones with the balls start chasing the ones who do not have a ball. Sometimes it is fun to give the runners (those without a ball) a 5 seconds head start before sending the ones with ball after them. The objective of the game is to not get caught holding a ball. If a student has a ball they have to chase down another player and tag or throw the ball at them. If the ball hits the player shoulders to feet then they have possession of the ball.

The runners can only go one direction on the track. The teacher can change that direction by giving a signal-I recommend two whistles-so that the runners are running into a ball instead of running away from it. Those with a ball can run either direction on the track to try and get rid of the ball. If you want to give them even more of an advantage then let then run across the field to quickly get to the other side (I make them stay on a white line (football markings) to do it though). If a player with a ball throws and misses the target they still have possession of that ball and must go get it. A player in possession of a ball can not get tagged so they have 2 dodgeballs to carry.

The reason students do not want to have a ball is that on the signal from the teacher-use one whistle-they have to do 5 push ups. This makes the students really work to get rid of a ball. If a player gets hit with a ball they have to do 2 push ups before trying to tag someone else.

This is a great game to work on fitness. All students will get a great cardiovascular workout and most will end up doing some push ups for upper body strength.

Diagram #15

Cross Country Dodgeball

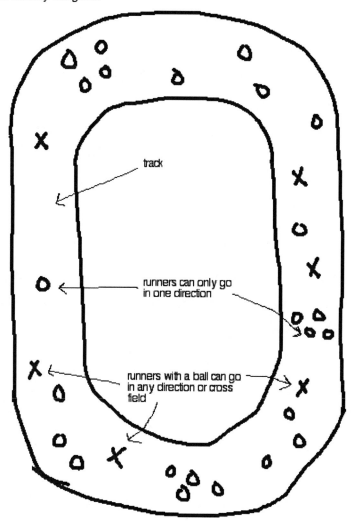

track

runners can only go
in one direction

runners with a ball can go
in any direction or cross
field

Tournament Dodgeball

While searching the internet I came across two organizations dedicated to dodgeball. What each has done is set up a system of play that is run as a tournament. Competition takes place at various times during the year depending on which organization sponsors it. The following two games are taken from each respective organization. I have played both with my 8th grade students and have had tremendous success. Please visit each web site for more information on joining the organization, playing in the tournaments, dodgeball rules and general fun facts about dodgeball.

The World Dodgeball Association

Equipment:

1 dodgeball, gymnasium with volleyball court markings or similar markings outside

Set Up:

This is a 7 on 7 format. Four players from each team will be inside their respective side of the court and the other 3 players will be on the outside of their opponents court. *(See Diagram 16)*

Play:

To start a game a referee will flip a coin to decide who gets the ball first. Like other dodgeball games the basic rules apply. If a player is hit shoulders to feet they are out. Catch a ball in the air and the thrower is out. Head shots do not count. But this game adds the fun element of passing to the game. Team "A" players may pass the ball to another player "A" who is on the opponents side of the court (out of bounds on the sides). This puts Team B players in a much better position to get hit.

Unique rules for this type of play are as follows. Floaters, those on the outside of the court, can not be eliminated by a hit. Dodgers, those inside the court, are the only one who can be knocked out. Dodgers from one team may intercept a ball to eliminate the thrower (can not be a floater). When all but 1 dodger remains a time out is called and the 3 floater become dodgers. When only 1 dodger is left for any team the opposing team may cross the center line up to the 10 ft. line. Any player, floater or dodger, who crosses a boundary line is eliminated from the game. Any player who holds a ball for more than 10 seconds is eliminated.

The other fun thing about this game is a scoring system has been established. The winning team earns points for the number of players left on the court. So if the winning team has 2 players left then they earn 2 points for their team. This is a good way to increase competitiveness because you can say the team with the most points at the end of the tourney wins. The number of wins alone may not be enough to win the tournament.

For more information please visit www.worlddodgeball. com. The web site has a ton of interesting items on it including press releases. The World Dodgeball Association is based out of Chicago, Illinois.

Hint:

When playing this game be sure to stress to your students that catching the ball is going to be a necessity if they do not want to lose right away. This game really is about gaining possession of the ball and keeping it for a s long as possible.

Diagram #16

The *World Dodgeball Association*
Formation

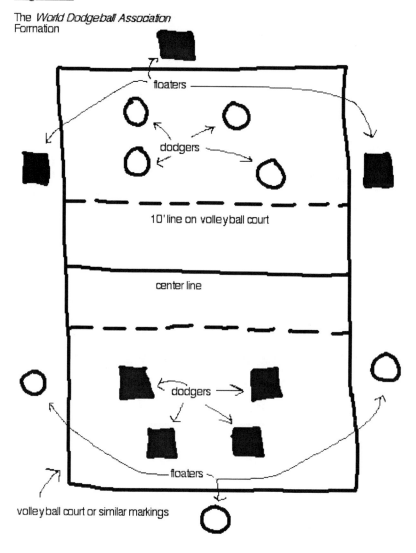

floaters

dodgers

10' line on volleyball court

center line

dodgers

floaters

volleyball court or similar markings

The National Amateur Dodgeball Association (NADA)

Equipment:

6 dodgeballs, a court or playing surface with volleyball court markings

Set Up:

This will be a 6 on 6 set up, each team using half of the court. The balls should be placed on the center line, 3 on one half and 3 on the other. *(See Diagram 17)*

Play:

One the signal from a referee play begins. Players may start by running to gain possession of the balls. Each team may only get the 3 balls to the right of the center of the court (fair start). The balls must be carried or rolled behind a 10' line before they can be thrown to get someone out.

Normal dodgeball rules apply in this game. If a player is hit shoulders to feet they are out. Head shots do not count. If a ball is caught then the thrower is out. Any player who steps over the center line or the side lines is out. A player may not step over the end line unless they are retrieving a ball from out-of-bounds/ no play area. If a player is getting a ball that is out of play they must exit the court by the end line and reenter the court by the same end line. Out players go behind or to the side of the court and may not get back in the game. First team to get all other opponents out wins.

Unique to this game is a rule about using a ball to block another ball. It is legal to hold a ball to block another thrown ball, but if that ball is knocked out of hands of the blocker then he/she is out.

Substitutions are permitted for injured players, but each team only has 2 time-outs to use.

While I never needed to put a time limit on games because they do go pretty fast, the NADA sets a 7 minute time limit for games. If there is no winner at the end of 7 minutes the team with the most players left wins. In case teams have equal an equal number of players left then a sudden death scenario in put in effect-the first team to get an opponent out wins.

Hint:

Your students will love playing this game. It moves real fast and gets quite competitive. To make it more interesting I put in the "2 Player Swing" rule-the same one used in the move *Dodgeball*. Here is how it works: if a player from team A catches a ball thrown by team B, the thrower from team B is "out". An "out" player from team A can now reenter the game (hence the 2 Player Swing, 1 out and 1 in). Have "out" players line up in the order they got out so you know the order they should reenter the game.

For more information please visit the National Amateur Dodgeball Association's web site at www.dodgeballusa.com.

Diagram #17

The *National Amateur Dodgeball Association* Formation

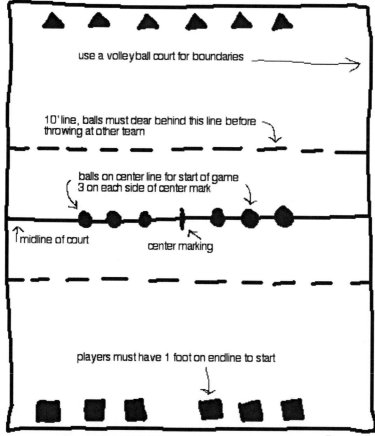

use a volleyball court for boundaries

10' line, balls must clear behind this line before throwing at other team

balls on center line for start of game
3 on each side of center mark

midline of court

center marking

players must have 1 foot on endline to start

players can only exit the court thru the endline, they must re-enter thru the endline as well

Skills, Techniques and Strategies

Not that you would have to teach any of the skills and techniques list below, but they do make the games more interesting. Note that I have never taught any of the skills listed below, students will pick them up all by themselves and refine them. Of course you can always take one or two and have students put them into a game to practice, but you will probably find it to be unnecessary.

1. "The Over-Under Move"

A player has two balls, one in each hand. If the player is right handed-toss the ball in the left hand up high in the air at an opponent. This creates a distraction because the defensive player will think it is an easy catch to get the offensive player out. The offensive player can then throw the ball in the right hand directly at the defensive player. Switch throwing hands for a left handed player.

2. "The Bowling Maneuver"

This basically the same as the "Over-Under", except an offensive player will roll a ball instead of tossing it high in the air. Setting this move up is very important and really works best when there are only a few players left on one team and they do not have a lot of the balls. A defensive player will get eager to pick up any ball which will make them easier to get out.

3. "The Windmill"

An offensive player will have a ball in each hand. In this move they get as close to the center line as possible and throw both balls at the same time. It is not always effective but becomes confusing to the defensive player because they do not know which ball to concentrate on catching and which one to dodge.

4. "The Partner Attack"

In this move players from the same team will partner up to try and get an opponent out. The first partner will throw their ball in an attempt to deceive or distract an opponent. Immediately following the first throw the second partner, or however many have teamed up, will throw their balls at the same opponent. This is a move that requires cooperation between players and good coordination/ timing. It is really cool when it works.

5. "The Pump Fake"

An easy one to master. An offensive player will fake a hard throw at an opponent to get them moving. Once the defensive player has taken the bait the ball is thrown. It is really fun when the defensive player jumps or hits the floor because they know they were just faked out and about to be out. In my experience, players who fall for this tactic are always laughing when they get out. (That is what makes this game fun.)

6. "Charge"

Here is a tactic that students will probably figure out on their own. Basically a whole bunch gather together and each one has a ball. On a signal they all charge the center line and throw at the same time. The students seem to organize this one with no problem and can use it again and again because there is no deception that needs to take place. This works real well when there are only a few players left on a team and they are hard to get out.

7. "The Catch and Release"

This is a defensive move to get opponents out. Here a defensive player who is really good at catching simply sets them self up to get a ball thrown at them and catches the ball. As soon as they catch the ball they will get rid of it to catch another one. I have had students who have one games by simply catching balls and never throwing one at an opponent. I would like to see more players use this technique. Catching is an under rated advantage in dodgeball games.

8. "The Dances With Wolves Move" (from the movie)

A seldom used technique, except for a select few who are will to sacrifice for the team. A single player will run right along the center line, almost begging to be hit. They will have one ball and at some point launch it at an opponent. Strange at may seem it does work because opposing players get excited about the easy target and become targets themselves. Of course there is always the possibility the player will get out, but that does not seem to deter students from trying.

9. "The I'm A Tree, Try And Hit Me Move"

This is a strange move that students will learn all by themselves. When they are the last player on their team and the opposing team has to get them out they will go to the back of the playing area and not move. Surprisingly it works. I personally think that the player using this moves knows that they won't be able to do much else so why not make the other team work real hard at getting them out. Students seem to like this because they can laugh at how long it takes to get out.

10. "The Oops, Your Out Move"

This is actually a mistake made by one offensive player who has not mastered the art of throwing with opposition. They intend to throw at one player, but because they do not use proper throwing techniques (step with the left foot if throwing with the right hand) they end up hitting someone else altogether. You have to laugh when it happens.

11. "The Sneak Attack"

This is a great deceptive throw. A player has to do a good job of setting this up. The best way to set another player up is to point and charge at them. They will think that they are the intended person to receive the throw. But at the last second the thrower will change position at throw at another unsuspecting player altogether. If it is set up right it almost always works. If you (the teacher) are playing with your students I highly recommend using it. It teaches students to always be aware of what is going on around them, in other words-pay attention!

12. "The Use Another Teammate As a Shield Move", also know as "Peek-A-Boo"

This is a funny one made famous from the movie "Dodgeball". One player will hide behind another player and use them as a shield and pop out every so often and make a throw. It does work even if the "shielding" player gets hit the "hiding" player still has a ball and can make a throw or move and hide behind someone else.

13. "The 'Grenade!' Move"

This is the funniest move I have ever witnessed. A player with a ball will be moving toward an opponent who also has a ball. The opponent will make their throw and then the other player hits and rolls on the floor (hence the grenade name) and then jumps up and throws their ball. It is so funny to watch students perform this move and even better when it works.

Opposition to the Opposition's Position

So what do those who are opposed to Dodgeball say about the game? Ironically they say the same thing about any game that has elements of competition. To summarize-it is the position of those who do not like dodgeball that "there are other games that teach the same skills". "It is to violent." "I am a teacher not a recreation leader." These are the statements of other Physical Educators and those who somehow are associated with the game. So let's take a moment to address some of these issues.

I would like to begin with the skills argument. Sure-there are other ways of teaching skills like catching and throwing. And there are a whole bunch of activities that teach balance, coordination and agility. You can always substitute one thing for something else. How about changing the rule allowing tackling in football to a two hand touch only rule. Do you think that football will remain the most popular sport in America. And we could make it a rule that pitchers in baseball can not throw the ball any faster than say 20 miles per hours. That would certainly make it easier for hitters-but would the pitchers be in any more danger? Maybe we should only use wiffle balls and bats in the MLB, that would make it safer for everyone; players, umpires, managers, fans and even the peanut guy.

Sounds ridiculous doesn't it? Of course it does. And why does it sound so ridiculous-because it makes no common sense to change accepted sports to make them safer. The fans do not want the game to change (and that is where the majority of money for major league sports comes from), the players do not want to change anything-they play the game because they like it the way it is, the owners do not want to change anything except to examine ways of making more money and the list can go on and on.

Dodgeball is a sport that is gaining acceptance across America. The movie of course has a lot to with it, but I also believe that people are just looking for something fun to do that does not fit into the traditional mold of acceptable sports. In my home town alone (and my area is a bit behind the times, other cities have already established formal leagues) I know of two major fitness centers that have added dodgeball leagues, and they are packed. One has it set up so anyone can come in and play and the other has people sign up in teams like a softball league. Area high schools are using dodgeball tournaments as fund raisers for charities. What is interesting is that these same schools have banned playing dodgeball in physical education, but allow it for a charity (?). Even more interesting is that the schools were swarmed with eager participants- students and teachers. (Does it strike anyone as unusual that a district would not allow a game to played in a supervised gym with trained experts but allows students to organize that same game for charity and play it in the gym?) The schools that I know of that have used dodgeball for charity have had tremendous success and raised a lot of money for a good cause and none had any casualties.

Look at sports trends in America. More and more of our youth are flocking to "extreme" sports like inline skating, snow boarding, street hockey, bmx biking, motto X style riding, mountain biking, rock climbing and so on and so on. Why? I asked some of my students who would be classified as "skateboarders" why they chose to be at the local skate park instead of on a football field or in a gym learning more traditional sports. The response was a simple one- today's sport programs are too "controlled by adults, with too many rules". All they were interested in was skating for the fun of it. Challenging themselves, pushing limits set by themselves and judging each other because, as they put it, "We are the experts at what we do." An interesting point. Putting dodgeball into the mix would make sense because it is a simple game to play that require no advanced sport skill. It also explains why I can get an entire class to play any dodgeball game, but not the same result with basketball. It is a simple fact that kids today like to play games that are simple, fast paced and not over loaded with rules.

So you are still not convinced. I will try one last comparison and leave it at that. If you are still not convinced that dodgeball would make a perfect addition to any sports curriculum or program then so be it.

How does Dodgeball compare to religion? I use this comparison any time the topic comes up and someone wants to discuss the merits of dodgeball with me. I know it may sound weird but read through it and see what you think. I promise to not turn it into a lecture on religions of the world and how it compares to Dodgeball-I'll keep it simple.

To me, any sport is like any religion you would find any where in the world. There are many different types of religions in our world today. It would be impossible to say any one is better than another, more directly, it would be wrong to say one was better. Sure, you have people from one specific religion tell you their's is the best and they may even be able to site specifics as to why. Wars have been waged over territories based upon religious beliefs (the Crusades for example), and even today people fight for control of an area of land that is based upon perceived religious borders. (The Middle East is a prime example.) But is any one of those religions better than another?

I am not a religious scholar. But I do know this; if any religion can make you a better person, it is a good set of beliefs to have. As long as you are not out killing on behalf of one religion than I say it is good for you and the world. So if any religious belief can make a happier, more well adjusted person why fight it? Go with it and enjoy the experience. Sport is the same thing.

If dodgeball or any other sport can make a stronger, healthier person than why fight it. Roll with it and enjoy the benefits- a stronger body, lower rates of obesity in our nations youth, lower rates of Type II Diabetes, people that live longer, happier children, less visits to the doctor's office, better academic performance in schools from elementary to college (studies have shown that an increase in the amount of physical activity a student gets in a day increases academic performance in both the classroom and on standardized tests), and perhaps the most important reason of all, people develop a healthy habit of staying physically active their whole life.

Final Thoughts

Hopefully I have given you something to think about. Even better would be if you tried out some of the games listed and changed them to fit your needs. If you are still skeptical please try playing the games <u>with</u> your students. You may find that you yourself have a renewed interest in a game that kids love and maybe you enjoyed as a kid. You will also find that the students get more excited about playing with you-you become the challenge yourself and kids love that. Not only will you be able to see how much fun they are having, you will gain a greater perspective of their actual physical abilities.

The most important thing to keep in mind when playing any dodgeball game is that it is the teacher who makes the game work, not the students. If any class, school or district that has had problems with dodgeball it is because the one in charge did not do a good job of ensuring all safety precautions were taken and students practice good social skills (sportsmanship). Solve problems as they occur and prevent them from happening next time by learning from mistakes. Coaches in football do this, as does any coach. (Where do you think the current helmet used in football comes from-trial and error and learning.)

And let us not forget-**Have fun!** If you enjoy what you are doing your students will also.

About The Author

I recieved a teaching degree in Health and Physical Education from Captial University in Columbus, Ohio. I am currently working on a Master's dregree in Sport Sciences from Ashland University. I teach Health and Physical Education at a middle school in central Ohio. I am also an American Red Cross instructor. I teach Lifeguard Training, Water Safety Instruction, First Aid, CPR and AED Administration.

I have spent the better part of my life learning and teaching about how to best be safe and maintain a safe environment for everyone's enjoyment. Whether that is in a classroom, a gym or at a pool, safety is my first priority. I took a great amount of time to write this book so that I would purposefully not include anything that I personally felt was an unsafe or would be an unsafe situation for students. Not only have I developed a lot of the games, with the help of my fellow teaching staff, I have played every game within this book with my students to see for myself how it played out. If I felt that any game listed in this book was unsafe to be a part of I would not have included it. It is the teacher that makes a game safe or unsafe-not the students/ players.

I myself am nothing more than a student learning from my students. I have watched and listened to them very intently to create games and movement units that they will not only enjoy but gain needed health benefits from. The students love the game of Dodgeball and I have seen how hard they work at playing the game.

I hope you enjoy the book and have as much success with Dodgeball as I have.

CPSIA information can be obtained at www.ICGtesting.com
Printed in the USA
BVOW032206290113

311924BV00002B/115/A

CO-PARENTING
Sharing Your Child Equally